Going to Britain

Eva Merk
Reinhard Leidig

Going to Britain

A handbook for young adults going on
school exchanges and trips to Britain

Ernst Klett Sprachen
Stuttgart

Bildquellennachweis
Fotolia LLC, New York: ©, **S. 43;** (Kaarsten), **S. 17;** (Oliver Hauptstock), **S. 47;** (Wogi), **S. 19;** Getty Images RF, München, **S. 49;** (skvoor), **S. 18;** Wilhelm-Bracke-Gesamtschule, Braunschweig: (Eva Merk), **S. 31;** (Reinhard Leidig), **S. 7, S. 16, S. 20, S. 23, S. 33, S. 40**

1. Auflage   1 ¹⁴ ¹³ ¹² ¹¹ ¹⁰ | 2027 26 25 24 23

Redaktion: Paul Newcomb
Layoutkonzeption: Elmar Feuerbach
Illustrationen: Johanna Seipelt, Braunschweig
Gestaltung und Satz: Eva Mokhlis, Swabianmedia, Stuttgart
Umschlaggestaltung: Elmar Feuerbach
Titelbild: shutterstock, New York, NY (Arid Ocean)
Druck und Bindung: Digitaldruck Tebben GmbH, Biessenhofen

Printed in Germany
ISBN 978-3-12-532701-6

Inhaltsverzeichnis

Introduction

So, you're going on a trip to Britain? Great! Exciting, isn't it? This book will help you to be well prepared for your trip or exchange. You will enjoy the time abroad even more if you feel sure about what to say in different situations.

Before your trip

Work through the book and complete the pages where necessary. This will help you to remember basic words and phrases that you need for everyday communication. Sometimes you are asked to find photographs and stick them into your book. This will help you show your host family where and how you live and what your family looks like, etc.

During your trip

This book is a language guide. Fill in the diary pages every day, collect small souvenirs such as tickets or photos and stick them into the scrapbook at the back of the book. Note down addresses, telephone numbers and e-mail addresses of people you meet and want to keep in touch with.

After your trip

Note down words that you want to remember. Stick in photographs of your trip, and you will have a souvenir which you can keep for ever!
Have a nice trip!

1. ME / US

About me

Name: ....

Address: ....

....

....

Tel.: ....

Mobile phone: ....

Date of birth: ....

Place of birth: ....

Nationality: ....

Passport (ID) Number: ....

My photo

Languages I speak or understand: ....

....

Colour of my hair: ....

Colour of my eyes: ....

Height: ....

Nickname: ....

Hobbies: ....

My village / town / city

Name: ....

Federal state: ....

Number of inhabitants: ....

Beautiful buildings: ....

What would you show to a visitor? Use the space below for drawings or photos.

About my school

Name: ....

Address: ....

....

....

E-Mail: ....

Tel.: ....

Number of pupils: .... Number of staff: ....

My form: .... Number of lessons per day: ....

First lesson starts at: .... Last lesson finishes at: ....

Name of head teacher ....

Form teacher(s): ....

Languages you can learn: ....

My favourite subjects: ....

What I like best: ....

What I don't like: ....

Stick a picture of your school here

My timetable

Times of lessons	Monday	Tuesday	Wednesday	Thursday	Friday

Maths – Science – English – German – French – Spanish – Latin – Russian – Art – Music – Geography – History – Social Studies – Information Technology – Technology – PE – RE – Drama - Club

Our group

Stick a picture of your group here

Names

Names of girls: ....

....

....

....

....

....

Names of boys: ....

....

....

....

....

A family

Henry and Diana

Rosemary   Helen and Andy   Ben and Sandy   George

Oliver and Emily   Sarah and Peter

1. Emily is Oliver's .... Oliver is Emily's ....

2. Emily is Helen's and Andy's .... Oliver is their ....

3. Helen and Andy are Emily's and Oliver's ....

4. Helen is Andy's .... and Emily's and Oliver's ....

5. Andy is Helen's .... and Emily's and Oliver's ....

6. Emily and Oliver are ....

7. Rosemary and Sandy are Emily's and Oliver's ....

8. George and Ben are Emily's and Oliver's ....

9. Emily is Rosemary's ....

10. Oliver is her ....

11. Sarah and Peter are Emily's and Oliver's ....

12. Emily is Henry's .... , Oliver is his ....

13. Henry is Emily's .... , Diana is her ....

14. Henry and Diana are Emily's and Oliver's ....

Look at the family tree on the opposite/previous page and finish the sentences.

Emily is Peter's .... Sandy is Emily's .... George is Emily's .... Oliver is Rosemary's .... Diana is Peter's .... Henry is Emily's .... Sarah is Ben's .... Emily is Ben's .... Helen is Andy's .... Ben is Sandy's ....

My family

Stick in a photograph of your family and write a few sentences about them (their names, ages, etc).

....

....

....

....

....

....

underwear

blouse

T-shirts

sunglasses

sweater

trainers

shorts

tights

swimwear

tights

dress

adapter

passport

money

boots

belt

writing material

trousers

gloves

umbrella

jacket

scarf

shoes

jeans

dictionary

skirt

socks

camera

soap

present

toothbrush

toothpaste

My packing list

Make a list of the things to pack and take with you.

1. .... 2. ....

3. .... 4. ....

5. .... 6. ....

7. .... 8. ....

9. .... 10. ....

11. .... 12. ....

13. .... 14. ....

15. .... 16. ....

17. .... 18. ....

19. .... 20. ....

21. .... 22. ....

23. .... 24. ....

25. .... 26. ....

Choose five items and explain why you will take them.

1. I'll take an electrical adapter to charge my mobile. ....

2. ....

3. ....

4. ....

5. ....

6. ....

2. Geography

Europe

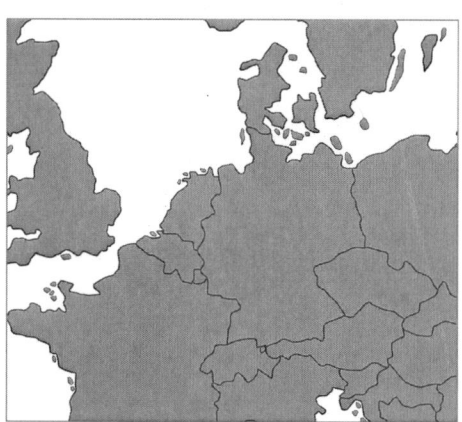

Which nine countries share a border with Germany?

1. ....   2. ....

3. ....   4. ....

5. ....   6. ....

7. ....   8. ....

9. ....

Find the English names for:

Mittelmeer: ....

Nordsee: ....

Ostsee: ....

Languages in Europe

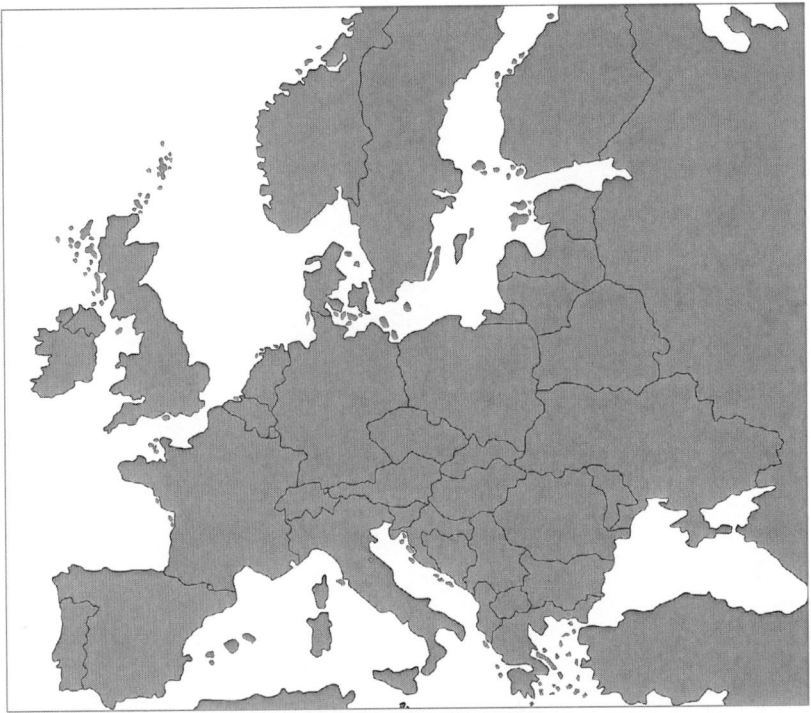

Where are these languages spoken? *Write the languages on the map.*

- German
- English
- French
- Irish
- Italian
- Polish

- Finnish
- Scottish
- Swedish
- Portuguese
- Norwegian
- Danish

- Spanish
- Russian
- Greek
- Dutch
- Turkish

The United Kingdom and Ireland

What are the capitals of ... ?

England ....

Scotland ....

Wales ....

Northern Ireland ....

Republic of Ireland ....

Mark the borders, name the countries and write in the capital cities.

Find the place where you are going to and write it on the map, too.

Germany

Find the English names for:

Hessen: .... Niedersachsen: ....

Bayern: .... Thüringen: ....

Nordrhein-Westfalen: ....

Rheinland-Pfalz: ....

Sachsen: .... Sachsen Anhalt: ....

3. My Partner

About my partner

Name: ....

Address: ....

....

....

E-Mail:

Tel.: ....

Mobile phone: ....

Date of birth: ....

Place of birth: ....

Languages he/she speaks or understands: ....

....

Colour of his/her hair: ....

Colour of his/her eyes: ....

Height: ....

Nickname: ....

Hobbies: ....

....

My partner's timetable

Time	Mon	Tues	Weds	Thurs	Fri

*Stick a picture of your
partner's room here*

This is my partner's room:

Which of these objects are in your partner's room? Mark them in the picture.

bed – bunk bed – lamp – wardrobe – chest of drawers – rug – picture –
poster – desk – chair – shelf – bookcase – table – chest – mirror – toys –
computer – radio – TV-set – game console – aquarium

4. My guest home and what to talk about when I'm there

Stick in a photograph of the house you live in.

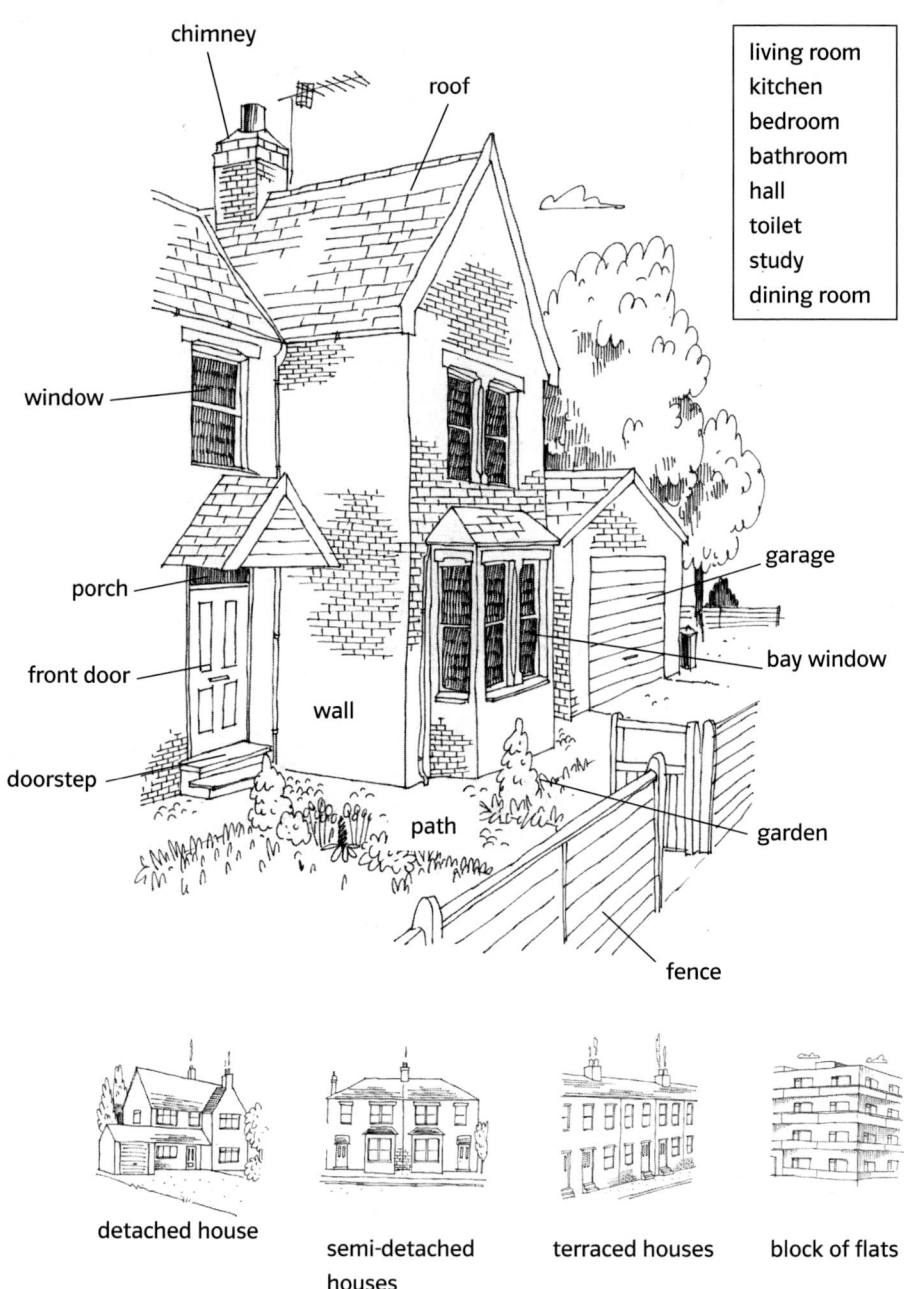

chimney

roof

living room
kitchen
bedroom
bathroom
hall
toilet
study
dining room

window

porch

front door

doorstep

wall

path

garden

garage

bay window

fence

detached house

semi-detached houses

terraced houses

block of flats

Describe your house or flat. (colour, garden, rooms, garage, shed, etc.)

....

....

....

....

....

....

Photos of your house or flat from inside

In the bathroom

Mark these objects with the numbers.

bath (1)

shower (3)

tap (2)

toilet (4)

washbasin (5)

soap (6)

toothbrush (7)

towel (8)

toothpaste (9)

sponge (10)

In the kitchen

Write down all the kitchen items that run on electricity: ....

....

....

....

....

....

Which of the items on page 27 would you use to make a good breakfast?

....

....

Right or wrong? Correct if necessary.

	Right	Wrong
1. You use the frying pan to make tea.	☐	☐
2. You need the washing-up liquid to make the cutlery clean.	☐	☐
3. A fridge is colder than a freezer.	☐	☐
4. You use a kettle to make hot water.	☐	☐
5. After the meal I put the dishes in the washing machine.	☐	☐
6. To open a tin I use a corkscrew.	☐	☐
7. I turn on the tap to get water.	☐	☐
8. You can warm up meals in the microwave oven.	☐	☐

....

....

....

....

....

....

Ask questions for these answers:

What you can ask:
- Where can I find a glass/plate/fork?
- Can I help with the cooking/washing-up?
- Where does this knife/fork/can opener go?
- Where shall I put the mugs/cups/the milk?

1. ....

- There's one in the drawer.

2. ....

- Please put it in the fridge.

3. ....

- Yes thanks. You can peel the potatoes.

4. ....

- Please leave them in the sink.

5. ....

- Yes thanks, you can dry the dishes.

Food and meals

What do you <u>like</u> ☺; what do you <u>not</u> like ☹?
Mark the fruits with one colour and the vegetables with a different one.

Talk about likes and dislikes

bananas	grapefruit	lettuce	grapes	cauliflower	apples
carrots	pumpkin	lemons	spinach	cucumber	
beans	cherries	apricots	cabbage	melon	peas
pineapple	tomatoes	peaches	strawberries		
oranges	plums	mushrooms	raspberries		

I like .... better than ....

I prefer .... to ....

I think .... is / are delicious.

I don't really like ....

cheese	chicken	fish	sausages	yoghurt	potatoes
salad	sweets	chips	sandwiches	cereals	
scrambled eggs	fried eggs	boiled eggs	meat		
baked beans	pork	beef	lamb		

Telephoning

You might use your mobile phone, your host family's phone or a public phone. For a public phone you need coins or a (tele)phone card, which you can buy in supermarkets or other shops.

To call someone in Germany you dial 0049 before the number and leave out the "0" of the area code. To call someone in Britain from abroad you dial 0044.

My host family's telephone number: ....

Mobile: ....

My teacher's mobile phone number: ....

A telephone call to your partner

In Great Britain you usually say your telephone number, not your name, when you answer the phone.

Woman: six-eight four-double four
You: This is (name) from (town/city). Could I speak to (name), please?
Woman: I'm sorry, she's out at the moment, but I could give her a message.
You: Could you tell her that I'll ring her again at 6 o'clock, please?
Woman: I'll write that down, could you spell your name, please?

You:	....
Woman:	Could you say that again, please?
You:	....
Woman:	Alright, I'll make sure she gets the message.
You:	Thank you very much, good bye.

Was sagst du, wenn du...

1. etwas nicht richtig verstanden hast?

   ....

2. mit jemandem am Telefon sprechen möchtest?

   ....

3. du möchtest, dass einer seinen Namen buchstabiert?

   ....

4. möchtest, dass jemand eine Nachricht übermittelt?

   ....

5. dich in England am Telefon meldest?

   ....

Meeting your host family

Meeting your host family and having the first meal together are very exciting moments. It is very useful to know some suitable sentences in these situations. Practise the dialogues with a partner.

First meeting

Mrs Ingham: Hello, Kathrin, welcome to England.
Kathrin: Hello, thank you.
Mrs Ingham: Did you have a good journey?
Kathrin: Yes, thank you, I enjoyed it very much.
Mrs Ingham: Let me take your luggage, you must be very tired.
Kathrin: Thanks, that's very kind of you.

The first meal

Mrs Ingham: Kathrin, can you sit next to Lisa, please?
Kathrin: Thank you.
Mrs Ingham: We're having roast beef and Yorkshire pudding for dinner. I hope you'll like it.
Kathrin: It looks delicious, thank you.
Mrs Ingham: Would you like water, lemonade or orange juice?
Kathrin: Lemonade, please.
Mrs Ingham: Help yourself to the vegetables.
Kathrin: Thank you.

... ...

Mrs Ingham: Would you like some more meat?
Kathrin: No thank you, I'm completely full! It was really tasty. Can I please go upstairs and unpack?
Mrs Ingham: Of course you can. Would you like anything special for breakfast tomorrow morning?
Kathrin: Nothing special for me, thank you.
Mrs Ingham: OK, then we'll have toast, marmalade and cereals, as usual.

There might be little problems. Talk about them.

Kathrin:	Excuse me, but I can't find a towel.
Mrs Ingham:	Oh dear, I think I forgot to put one on your bed. I am sorry.
Kathrin:	No problem, thank you.

Mrs Ingham:	Have some strawberries with whipped cream. They are from our garden.
Kathrin:	I'm so sorry, but I can't eat them because I'm allergic to strawberries.
Mrs Ingham:	What a pity! Would you fancy some chocolate pudding or an ice-cream instead?
Kathrin:	Yummy, I love ice-cream. Thank you.

Kathrin:	Excuse me, please, I have got a problem. I wanted to charge my mobile, but it won't work.
Mr Ingham:	Let me have a look. You have your adapter, I see. Oh, but you haven't turned this little switch on!
Kathrin:	Oh, there's a switch, I didn't see, thanks.
Mr Ingham:	You're welcome.

Kathrin:	I don't feel well this morning. I've got a sore throat/stomach ache/headache/pain in my knee.
Mrs Ingham:	Let me have a look. … Hm, I'll have to get you some medicine from the chemist's.
Kathrin:	Oh, that's very kind of you. Thank you so much!

Useful phrases in the family

- Could I have a (*glass of orange juice*), please?
- Would you mind if I (*listened to some music*)?
- Excuse me, I'll be back in a minute.
- I'm a bit tired, I think I'll go to bed now. Good night.
- Could you help me with the (*telephone*), please?
- Thanks very much for your help.
- Sorry, but I don't think (*the lamp/the shower*) is working.
- Do you think you could (*collect me from/drop me off at*) the bus stop, please?
- Thank you, that would be lovely/nice.
- Would you like *rice or potatoes with the fish?*
- I don't mind, I like both.
- I like this food, it's really delicious.
- The *pizza* tastes great. You are a very good cook.
- I'm (quite) hungry/thirsty. / I'm full.
- Thank you for the lovely meal!

Was sagst du, wenn (du) ...

1. wissen möchtest, ob du Musik hören kannst?

   ....

2. müde bist und ins Bett gehen möchtest?

   ....

   ....

3. dich für eine Hilfe bedanken möchtest?

   ....

4. fragen möchtest, ob es möglich ist dich abzuholen?

   ....

   ....

5. sagen möchtest, dass es dir egal ist? (*Vorsicht: nicht:* "I don't care!")

....

6. ein Handtuch haben möchtest?

....

7. wenn dir das Essen schmeckt?

....

8. nur mal kurz aus dem Zimmer gehen willst?

....

9. wenn das Licht nicht funktioniert?

....

10. Hilfe beim Telefonieren brauchst?

....

What do you say in these situations?

Match the phrase to the situation.

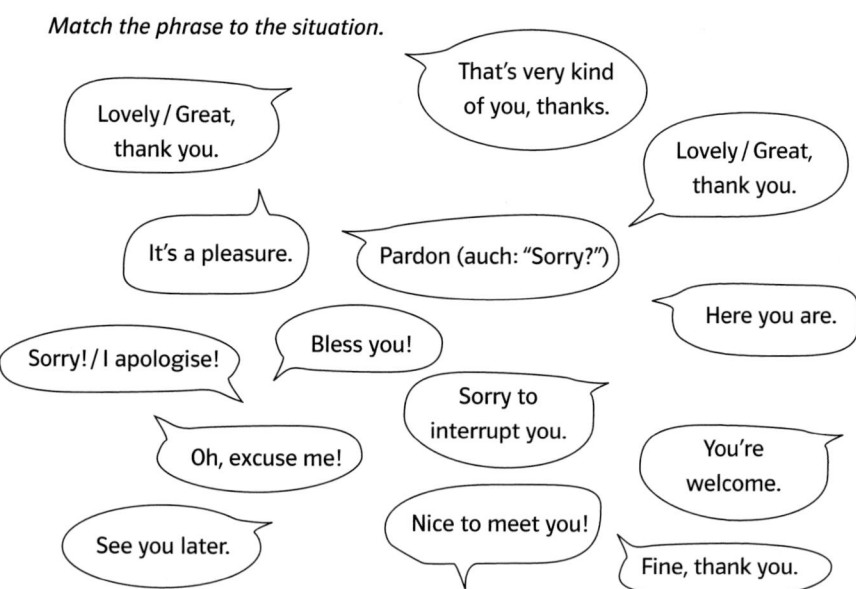

1. You didn't hear what somebody said: ....

2. You need to interrupt somebody: ....

3. Your friend sneezes *(niesen)*: ....

4. You sneeze: ....

5. You leave your host family in the morning: ....

6. A friend buys you an ice cream: ....

7. You meet the family's grandmother for the first time.

....

8. A friend asks you, "How are you?" ....

9. Could you pass me the salt, please? ....

10. After a nice day out your family ask you, "How was it?"

....

11. You give a present to your host family. They say, "Thank you."

....

12. The mother in your host family has washed all your clothes.

....

How are you today?

Thank you, I'm fine.
I'm very well, thanks
I don't feel very well.
I feel ill.
I've got a cold.
I've got a sore throat.
I've got a headache.
I've got toothache.
My shoulder is aching.

I feel sick.
I've got a temperature.
I've got hay fever.
Have you got an aspirin?
Have you got some medicine for me?
I need to go to the dentist.
Can you call a doctor, please?
I'd like to speak with my parents first.

Was sagst du, wenn du...

1. Zahnschmerzen hast? ....

2. Heuschnupfen hast? ....

3. dich ganz gesund fühlst? ....

4. Fieber hast? ....

5. zum Zahnarzt gehen möchtest? ....

6. möchtest, dass ein Arzt kommt? ....

7. Halsschmerzen hast? ....

8. dich krank fühlst? ....

What you do every day

Your host family or the teachers in your partner school may ask you to
introduce yourself and to tell them something about your family and your daily
routine. *Prepare a short talk!*

Say something about yourself

I usually get up at .... o'clock. I have a shower/bath in the morning/evening. At

the weekends I usually sleep until .... o'clock. I love ....

.... for breakfast. I go to school by .... / I walk to school.

It takes .... minutes. I have lunch in school. / I take sandwiches to school.

My favourite food is .... When I come home from

school first thing I usually do is (eat/drink/play) ....

.... We have .... pet(s). Usually we have our supper at ....

o'clock. My hobbies are ....•

At the weekends we often ....•

Before I go to sleep, I love to do/play/drink/eat/ read/watch ....

....•

My mum always/ never/usually ....

....•

My dad never/often/always ....

....•

My brother(s) / sister(s) ....

....•

Our neighbours ....

....•

We often/never/sometimes go to ....

....•

5. Out and about

Asking questions

Asking questions is very important. It helps you get information and keeps a conversation going.

I. Question words

Where?

How?

Why?

What?

Who?

When?

What time do you leave for school? **Where** can I buy video games? **When** do you usually go to bed? **Why** do you put vinegar on your chips? **How** do I open the window?

II. Do... / Don't... ?

Do you sell t-shirts? **Don't** you like mayonnaise on your chips? **Do** you like chocolate cake? **Do** you often go to the cinema? **Do** you want me to do anything?

III. Have... / Are... / Is... ?

Have you got a digital camera? **Have** you ever been to Italy? **Are** there any family rules I should know? **Is** it OK if I put this here? **Is** the front door locked?

IV. Can... / Could... / Would... (Being polite)

Can I use your computer, please? **Could** I check my e-mails, please? **Could** you help me to carry my bag upstairs, please? **Would** you mind if I opened the window? **Could** you pass me the salt, please?

Stelle folgende Fragen:

1. Wo ist deine Mutter? ....

2. Wann ist dein Geburtstag? ....

3. Wer ist dein Englischlehrer? ....

4. Was ist deine Lieblingsband? ....

5. Wie oft gehst du ins Kino? ....

6. Warum ist dein Hund so müde? ....

7. Nimmst du Zucker in deinen Tee? ....

8. Siehst du oft deine Großmutter? ....

....

9. Möchtest du fernsehen? ....

....

10. Isst du kein Fleisch? ....

11. Magst du Fisch? ....

12. Hast du ein Haustier? ....

13. Ist es in Ordnung, wenn ich um 8 Uhr aufstehe? ....
....

14. Ist ein Schokoladenpudding im Kühlschrank? ....
....

15. Sind die Teller im Geschirrspüler? ....
....

16. Sind die Hunde draußen? ....

17. Kann ich dir helfen? ....

18. Könntest du mir bitte helfen? ....

19. Würde es dir etwas ausmachen, wenn ich ins Bett gehe? ....
....

20. Möchtest du Tee oder Kaffee? ....
....

Pounds sterling

You buy a CD for £8.90 and a bar of chocolate for £2.50 and two postcards for 75p each.

1. How much do you have to pay? ....

2. You pay with a £20 note. How much change do you get?

   ....

3. What is the exchange rate now? €1 = £ ....

In a shop (1)

Put the dialogue into the correct order, then act it out with a partner.

Jenny: Yes, I'm looking for a pullover.	☐
Assistant: Thank you.	☐
Assistant: Yes, of course.	☐
Jenny: That's not too expensive. I'll take it.	☐
Jenny: Does the pullover look good on me?	☐
Assistant: And what about that pullover?	☐
Assistant: What size are you?	☐
Jenny: No, it is not my colour.	☐
Assistant: Good afternoon, can I help you?	1
Jenny: I fancy it! How much is it?	☐
Assistant: And do you like this red one?	☐
Jenny: Thank you, good bye.	☐
Jenny: No, it looks too big.	☐
Assistant: What about this yellow pullover?	☐
Assistant: It is only £13.	☐
Jenny: I'm usually size S.	☐
Jenny: Oh yes, I like red, it's my favourite colour. Can I try it on?	☐
Assistant: Oh yes, it does, it looks great!	☐

Some more useful phrases

too tight – too loose – too long – it doesn't fit – too expensive –
not exactly what I wanted – Thank you, I'm just looking

In a shop (2)

Read and act out this dialogue. When you have learned it, act it out with your book closed.

Assistant: Hello, can I help you?

Liam: I need a memory stick, please.

Assistant: We have a special offer here. These sticks are only £14.95.

Liam: How many gigabytes have they got?

Assistant: Um, two. Two gigabytes.

Liam: OK, I'll take one, please.

Assistant: Here you are. Please pay at the cash desk over there.

Liam: Thank you. Good bye.

Asking and telling someone the way

Useful phrases

Excuse me. – Can you tell me the way to...? – Go straight on – turn left/
right at... – bear left/right – the first/second turning on the left/right –
The ... is on the left/right – opposite the... – just past the... –
You can't miss it! – Thank you very much – You're welcome.

Examples:

Excuse me, can you tell me the way to the tube station please?

Yes, of course.

Go straight on to the traffic lights.

Turn left into The Grange.

The underground station is on the left, opposite the garage.

Thank you very much.

Excuse me please. Where is the bus stop for the 38, please?

Ok, you go down Station Road and turn right into High Street.

You will see the bus stop on your left, after the police station.

Thanks.

Tasks:

Ask for the way to a supermarket / a snack bar / the hospital / a bank.
Your partner will tell you the way.

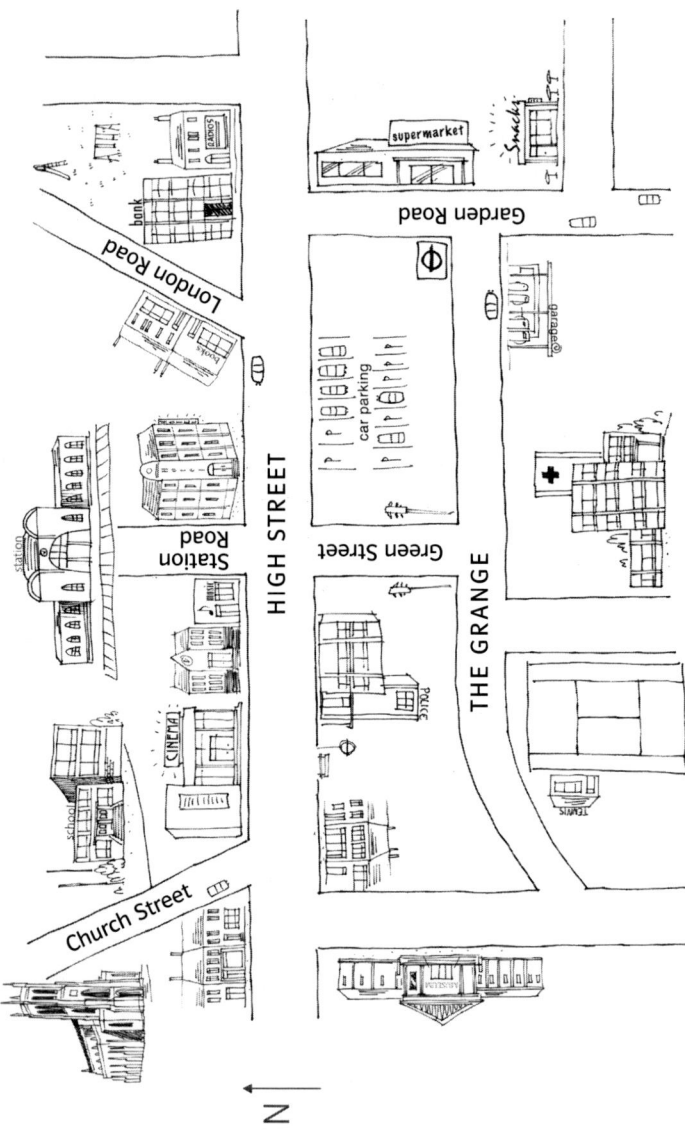

6. London

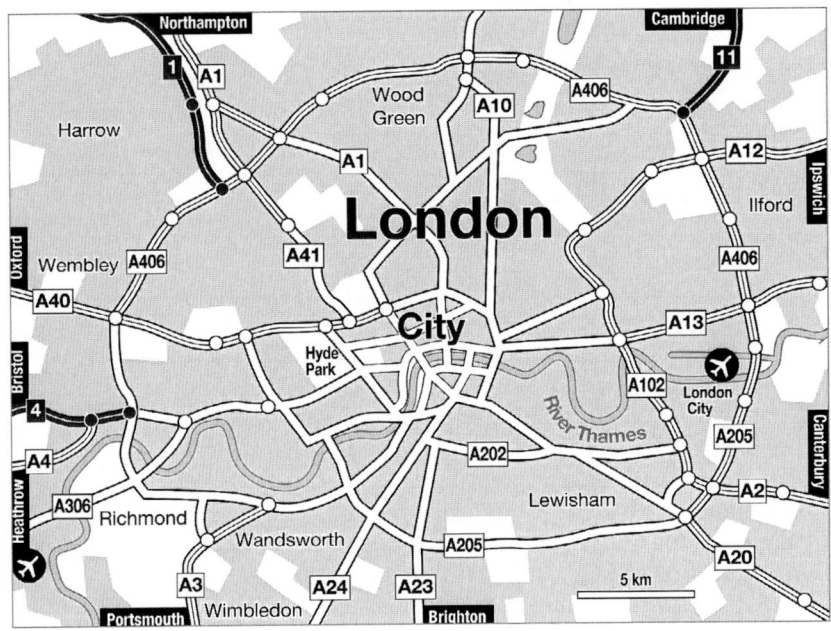

London sights

How was your trip to London?

excellent, expensive, interesting, scary, noisy, amazing, smashing, great, funny, picturesque, crowded, beautiful, cool, dangerous, impressive, huge, trendy, old fashioned, not bad, boring, breathtaking, good fun

Sights	Tick	How was it?
Buckingham Palace		
The Tower of London		
Tower Bridge		
The Houses of Parliament		
The British Museum		
St Paul's Cathedral		
Westminster Abbey		
Harrod's		
Madame Tussaud's		
The London Eye		
The Globe Theatre		
Oxford Street		
Piccadilly Circus		
Trafalgar Square		
Covent Garden		
Victoria Station		
The Tate Gallery		
The London Dungeon		
The Bank of England Museum		

On the underground

Find a London tube map online and plan your journey.

From OXFORD CIRCUS to VICTORIA:
Start at Oxford Circus, buy a ticket to Victoria. Take the VICTORIA LINE, SOUTHBOUND and get off at the **second** station.

From PICCADILLY CIRCUS to LIVERPOOL STREET:
Buy a ticket, follow the signs to the PICCADILLY LINE, NORTHBOUND. Change at KING'S CROSS onto the METROPOLITAN LINE, SOUTHBOUND and get off at the **fourth** station.

Complete the dialogue.
· Excuse me, please, how do I get to Tower Hill?
· Oh, that's easy. We are here at Oxford Circus.
· Take the .... Line eastbound to Bank. Follow the signs to Monument station, where you take the .... or Circle Line, eastbound and get off at the first station, Tower Hill.
· Thank you very much.

DIARY: Day 1

Day: .... Date: ....

My teacher's mobile phone: ....

Today's weather	Activities	Today I ate:
	Our journey: We started at .... We passed 	
	The journey took .... hours. In the evening	

What I bought. Where? Price?

....

I went to bed at ....

My new words of the day: ....

....

....

....

50

DIARY: Day 2

Day: .... **Date:** ....

Today's weather	Activities	Today I ate
	In the morning:	
	In the afternoon:	
	In the evening:	

What I bought. Where? Price?

....

I went to bed at ....

My new words of the day: ....

....

....

....

DIARY: Day 3

Day: .... **Date:** ....

Today's weather	Activities	Today I ate
	In the morning:	
	In the afternoon:	
	In the evening:	

What I bought. Where? Price?

....

I went to bed at ....

My new words of the day: ....

....

....

....

DIARY: Day 4

Day: .... **Date:** ....

Today's weather	Activities	Today I ate
	In the morning:	
	In the afternoon:	
	In the evening:	

What I bought. Where? Price?

....

I went to bed at ....

My new words of the day: ....

....

....

....

DIARY: Day 5

Day: .... Date: ....

Today's weather	Activities	Today I ate
	In the morning:	
	In the afternoon:	
	In the evening:	

What I bought. Where? Price?

....

I went to bed at ....

My new words of the day: ....

....

....

....

DIARY: Day 6

Day: .... **Date:** ....

Today's weather	Activities	Today I ate
	In the morning:	
	In the afternoon:	
	In the evening:	

What I bought. Where? Price?

....

I went to bed at ....

My new words of the day: ....

....

....

....

DIARY: Day 7

Day: .... **Date:** ....

Today's weather	Activities	Today I ate
	In the morning:	
	In the afternoon:	
	In the evening:	

What I bought. Where? Price?

....

I went to bed at ....

My new words of the day: ....

....

....

....

My scrapbook

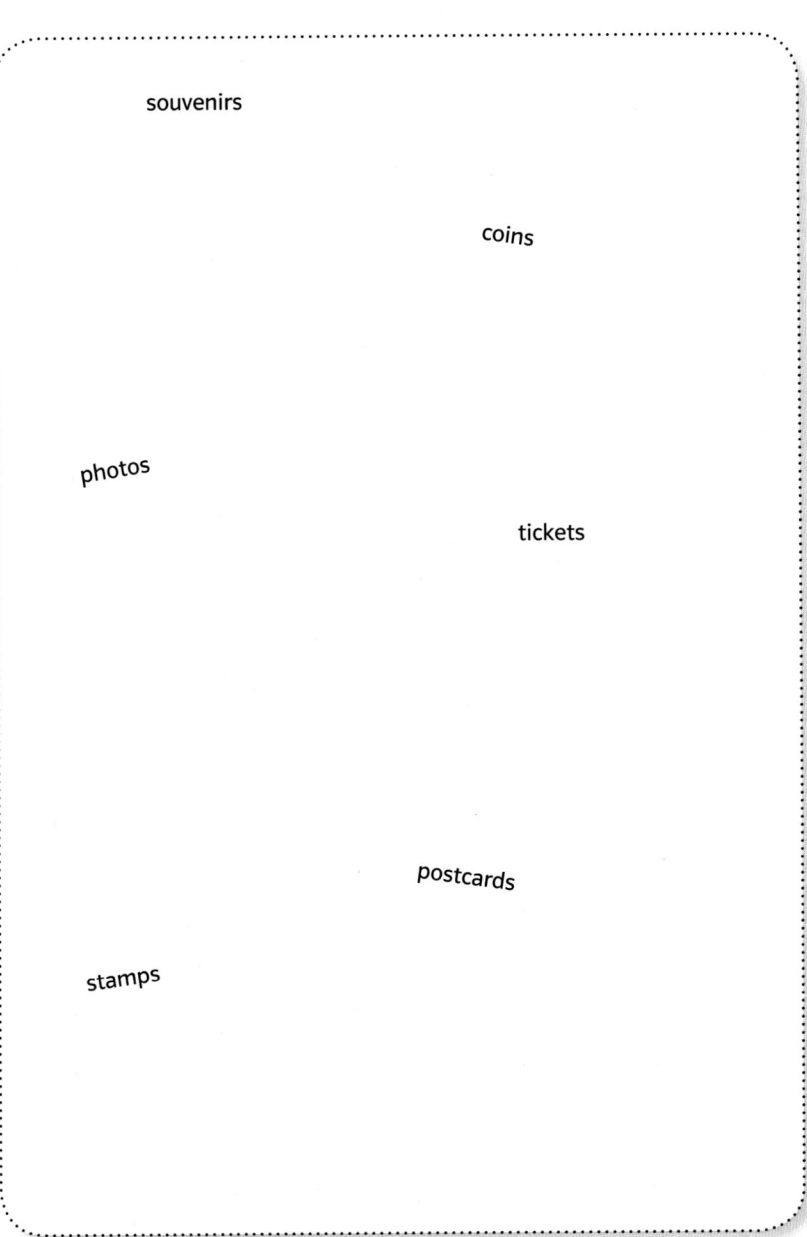

souvenirs

coins

photos

tickets

postcards

stamps

My scrapbook

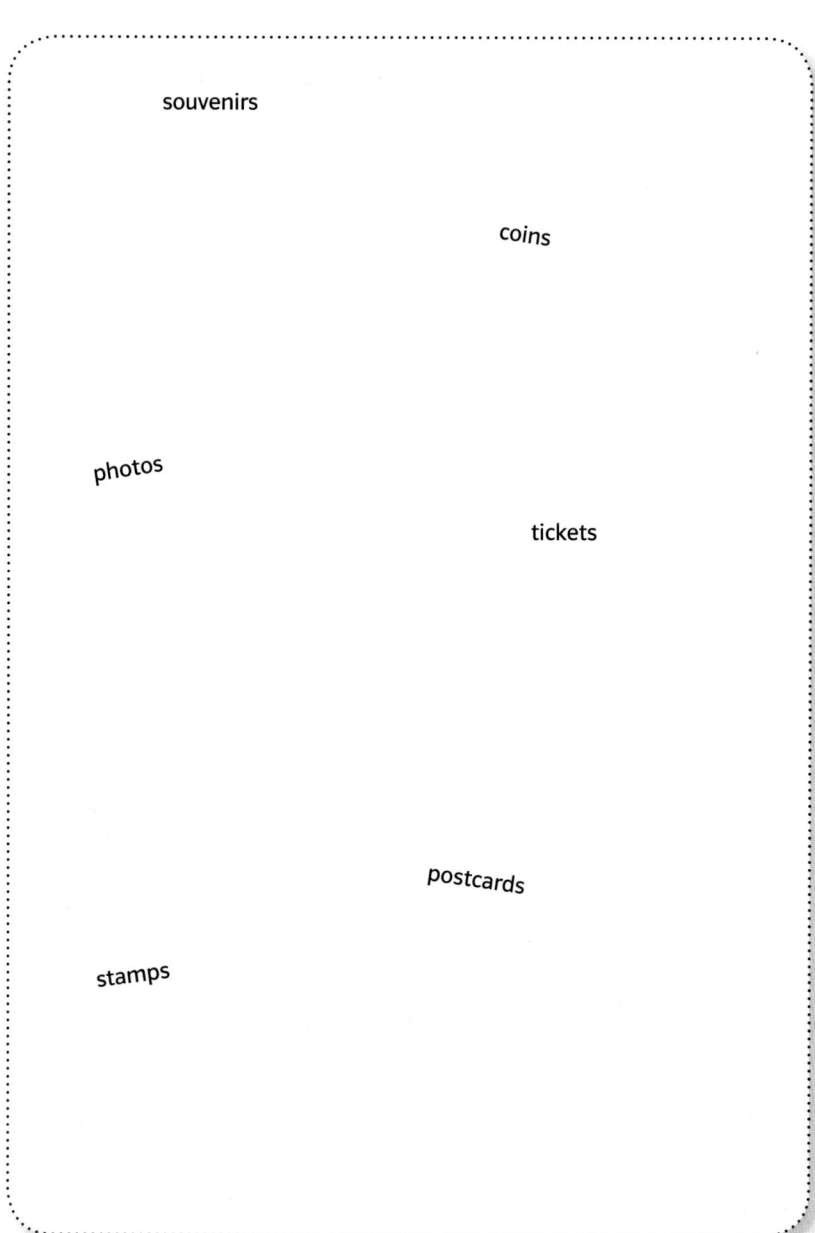

souvenirs

coins

photos

tickets

postcards

stamps

My scrapbook

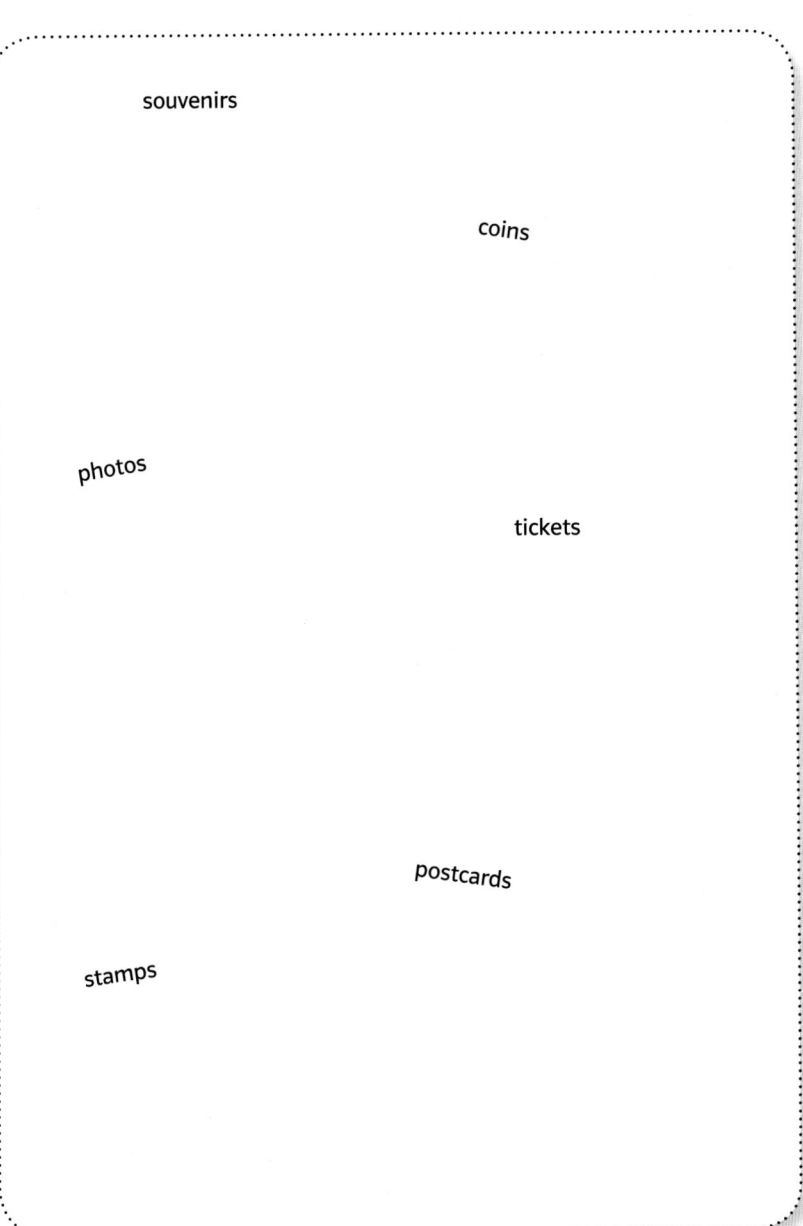

souvenirs

coins

photos

tickets

postcards

stamps

My scrapbook

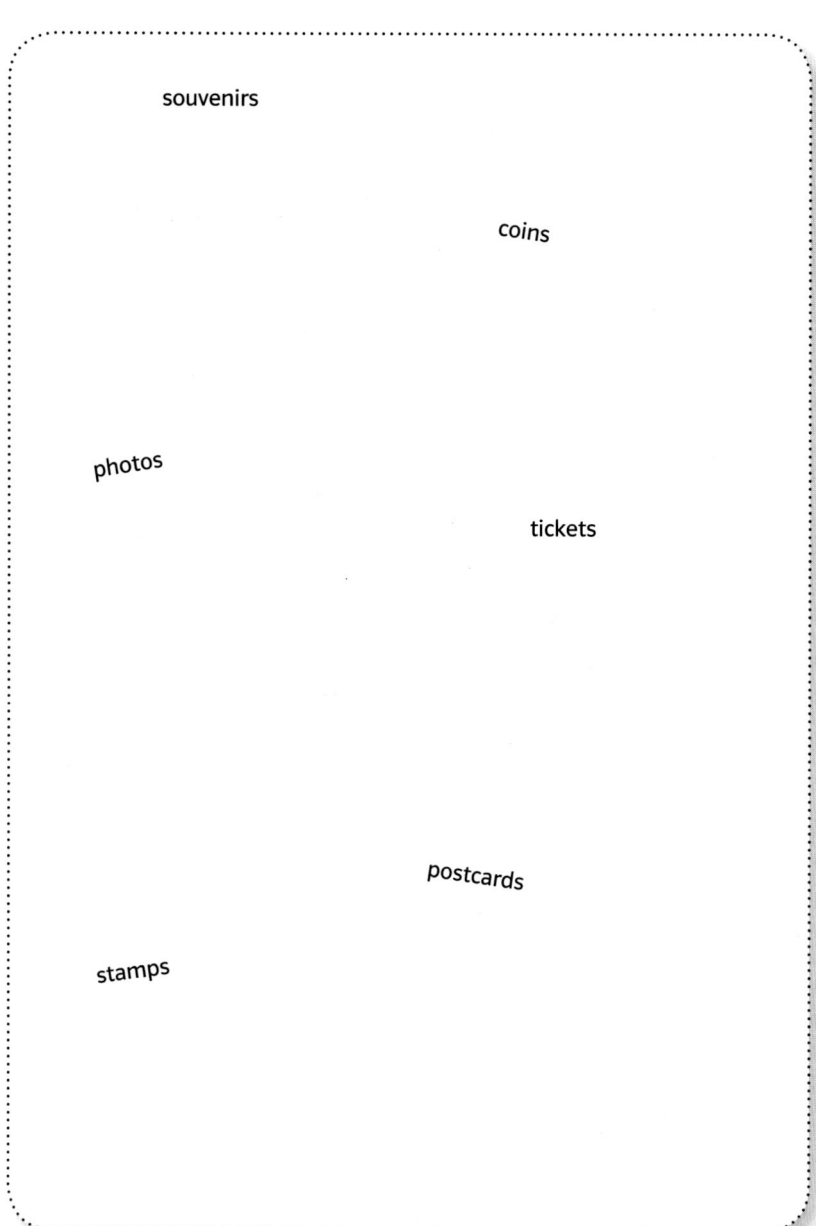

souvenirs

coins

photos

tickets

postcards

stamps

My scrapbook

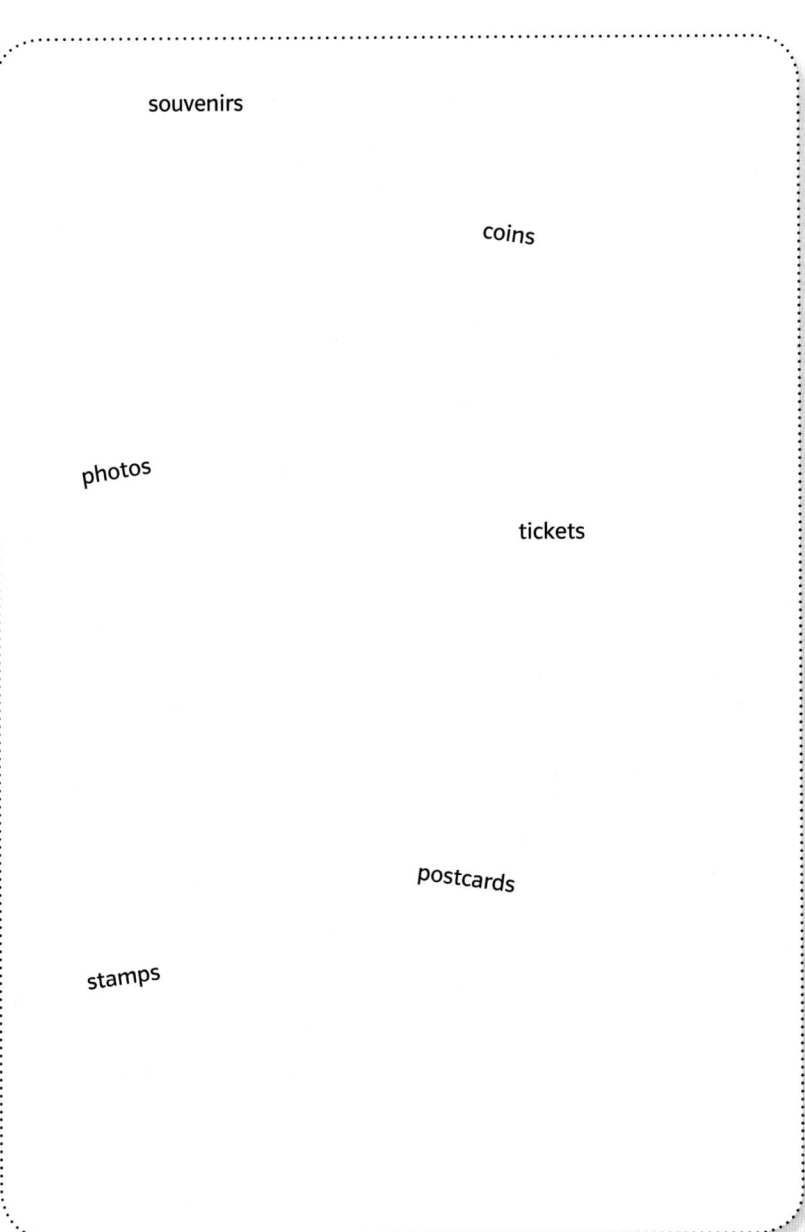

souvenirs

coins

photos

tickets

postcards

stamps

My contacts

Name	Address	Telephone / Mobile	e-mail address

Lösungen

S. 12 / 13 **A family:** 1. sister … brother. 2. daughter … son. 3. parents 4. wife … mother. 5. husband … father. 6. brother and sister / siblings 7. aunts. 8. uncles 9. niece. 10 nephew. 11. cousins. 12. granddaughter / grandchild … grandson / grandchild 13. grandfather / grandad / grandpa … grandmother / grandma. 14. grandparents

S. 13 cousin, aunt, uncle, nephew, grandmother, grandfather, daughter, niece, wife, husband

S. 16 / 17 **Europe:** France, Luxembourg, Belgium, The Netherlands, Denmark, Poland, The Czech Republic, Austria, Switzerland, The Mediterranean Sea, The North Sea, The Baltic Sea

S. 18 **The U.K. and Ireland:** London, Edinburgh, Cardiff, Belfast, Dublin

S. 19 **Germany:** Hesse, Lower Saxony, Bavaria, Thuringia, North Rhine-Westphalia, Rhineland-Palatinate, Saxony, Saxony-Anhalt

S. 26 **In the bathroom:** 1. Badewanne, 2. Wasserhahn, 3. Dusche, 4. Toilette, 5. Waschbecken, 6. Seife, 7. Zahnbürste, 8. Handtuch, 9. Zahnpasta, 10. Schwamm

S. 27 **In the kitchen:** dishwasher, freezer, fridge, oven, microwave, toaster, washing machine, kettle, mixer, tumble drier, iron

S. 28 **Right or wrong:** w, r, w, r, w, w, r, r
1. You use the teapot to make tea. 3. A freezer is colder than a fridge. 5. After the meal I put the dishes in the dish washer. 6. To open a tin I use a tin opener or can opener.

S. 29 **What you can ask:** 1. Where can I find a fork? 2. Where shall I put the milk? 3. Can I help with the cooking? 4. Where shall I put the cups? 5. Can I help with the washing up?

S. 32 **Was sagst du…** 1. Can you say that again, please? 2. Could I speak to …, please? 3. Could you spell your name, please? 4. Could you give her/him a message? 5. (Du sagst die Telefonnummer und nicht den Namen).

S. 35 **Useful phrases in the family:** 1. Would you mind if I listened to some music? 2. I'm a bit tired, I think I'll go to bed now. Good night. 3. Thanks very much for your help. 4. Do you think you could collect me, please? 5. I don't mind, I like both. 6. Could I have a towel, please? 7. I like this food. You are a great cook. (or) I like this food, it's really delicious. 8. Excuse me, I'll be back in a minute. 9. Sorry, but I don't think the light is working. 10. Could you help me with the telephone, please?

S. 36/37 **What do you say in these situations?** 1. Pardon? (or) Sorry? 2. Sorry to interrupt you. 3. Bless you! 4. Sorry! (or) I apologise! (or) Excuse me. 5. See you later. 6. Lovely / Great, thank you. 7. Nice to meet you. 8. Fine, thank you. 9. Here you are. 10. Lovely / Great, thank you. 11. It's a pleasure. (or) You are welcome. 12. That's very kind of you, thanks.

S. 38 **Was sagst du, wenn du . . . :** 1. I've got toothache. 2. I've got hay fever. 3. I'm very well, thanks. 4. I've got a temperature. 5. I need to go to the dentist. 6. Can you call a doctor, please? 7. I've got a sore throat. 8. I feel ill.

S. 41 **Stelle folgende Fragen:** 1. Where is your mother? 2. When is your birthday? 3. Who is your English teacher? 4. What is your favourite band? 5. How often do you go to the cinema? 6. Why is your dog so tired? 7. Do you take sugar in your tea? 8. Do you see your grandmother often? 9. Would you like to watch television? 10. Don't you eat (any) meat? 11. Do you like fish? 12. Have you got a pet? 13. Is it OK if I get up at 8 o'clock? 14. Is there any chocolate pudding in the fridge? 15. Are the dishes in the dishwasher? 16. Are the dogs outside? 17. Can I help you? 18. Could you help me, please? 19. Would you mind if I went to bed now? 20. Would you prefer (like) tea or coffee?

S. 43 **Pounds sterling:** 1. 12 pounds 90 pence 2. 7 pounds 10 pence

S. 44 **In a shop (1):** 2, 17, 11, 16, 12, 7, 3, 6, 1, 14, 9, 18, 8, 5, 15, 4, 10, 13

S. 49 **On the underground:** Central, District